Faith and Yosemite

Fourth Edition

Tunnel View, Thanksgiving Day Morning, 1963

James J. Stewart

Poetry and Images
© Copyright James J. Stewart

Fourth Edition
© Copyright 2018 James J. Stewart

ISBN: 978-1-7326609-0-8

Tree Moss

Vision

Vision is not limited to things the eye can see —

Vision also comes from wisdom born of what can be.

Others may insist on setting limits to their quests.

Those of faith believe for things that others only jest.

Sometimes vision comes from dreams

                or wishes in our hearts,

Others may awaken from a dream and have a start.

New beginnings have a path,

                and that's the key, you see.

If the dream has come from God,

                fulfillment's meant to be.

God has dreams for each of us

before we're in our womb.

Circumstances do not simply lead us to our tomb.

Dreams of God are planned to help us thrive,

                not just survive.

Life from God is meant to make us glad to be alive.

Vision then is born of hope, with faith

                that fuels our trust.

Vision's proof comes when fulfilled

                and skepticism's bust.

Dreams from God can be fulfilled,

                for God just cannot fail.

God fulfills through us His dreams

                and helps our spirits sail.

Path behind "The Ahwahnee" Hotel

Further Vision

Walking with our heads turned back,
        we see from whence we've come.
We try to learn from our mistakes —
        embarrassed, sometimes numb.
We strain to look into the past, as though
        salvation's there,
But we must then forgive ourselves
        to gain our future's share.

Sometimes we walk with eyes turned down,
        so not to stub our toe.
We think that walking carefully
        will save us future woe.
Ignoring what our future holds
        or whence our path has led,
We find that faith and hope are gone —
        we're like the living dead.

It's hard to lift our eyes to see —
        ahead seems cold and dark.
Our logic's eyes won't let us see
        what trusting sees "by heart."

The holy light makes future bright
        for those who walk with God —
With hearts illumined by the Christ,
        the angels then applaud.

It's not that homework's easy
        for a healthy walk with Him —
It's just without the light of Christ
        the future's mighty dim.
The eyes with which our hearts can see
        require a fertile mind.
Imagination's holy gift
        sees faith's great treasure find.

If you will dare to look with me
        where God would have us see,
I think we'll find the future
        of the church that is to be.
It's risky, yes, to follow eyes of heart
        with trusting love,
But heart's reward is pow'r unleashed —
        and joy in heav'n above!

Historic Yosemite Chapel

Christmas Images

What is the image that we want to see?
What's in the mirror that we want to be?
Yesterday's heroes are not what we want,
Our precious egos' what we want to flaunt.
'Me' generation and me on the line.
'Me' for self-help so more me we can chime.

Who are our heroes and who seeks the fame?
Heroes in everyone, that is our game.
Even in church, we find much of the same,
Self-esteem's hype is a Christian's cocaine.
Charges so strong are not gentle to hear.
Being a sheep seems like self-esteem's smear.

Di'gnosis is painful and yet there is hope.
Hope springs eternal and more for God's "dopes."
Setting their hopes on that bright Christmas star,
Brought "home" some "wise" men
                    who came from afar.

Manger's sweet wisdom made theirs into waste,
Hope born of woman so young and so chaste.
Hope also flowed from
            some shepherds, who came,
Listening to God who had called all the same:
"Leave now your flocks and come now into town—
Meet now your shepherd
            and worship bowed down."
They wanted care being known who they were,
Found care in him knowing just whose they were.

See in the manger the image of God,
Then see your mirror and be truly awed.
Yes, we are made in that image and more.
"Image" but not the true God, just a door.
If, when you're opened there's love there to see,
Then you are who God's created to be.

'Me' Generation, O people take note,
Salvation's ours, but it's not by our vote!
Self-help is out, only fools will defend--
Death brings helplessness to this life's end.
There are no keys found in riches or lands--
All the control is in God's mighty hands.

Christ is the firstborn of all human race,
Rebirth begins seeing Christ's baby face,
Which is confirmed in the empty tomb's grace.
Image of God, we have found our home base,
Nurtured in swaddling cloths rather than lace.
Walk with him, talk with him, now, face to face.

Yosemite Falls, seen from "Swinging" Bridge

Friends

Friends are those who share our joys,
        our sorrows, and our pains.
No one but a friend remembers
        long lost Jacks and Janes.
Closest friends just listen when
        we're bursting at our seams —
Only friends can help us mend
        the shards of broken dreams.
Keeping friends is harder
        than is making friends, you know.
Nurture is essential to maintain
        a friendship's flow.
Sometimes years go by with all the efforts
        on one side —
Then the times can change, and efforts
        flow back like the tide.
My best friend puts up with me through
        good times and through bad.
There's been times when I've brought pain
        and truly made him sad.

In the past, I've sometimes
        spoken carelessly to him.
There've been moments when I've stretched
        our friendship mighty thin.
There've been times I've made a mess
        and tried to shift the blame.

He's been patient through the worst,
        our friendship's been the same.
All too easily I think I'm doing all I can.
I must face the fact I'm not
        a perfect working man!
All of this is leading to a very simple fact.
Friendship's best comes not from us
        but is divinely backed.
My best friend is my Redeemer,
        Master, Teacher, Lord!
Serving God in Jesus' name
        is friendship's grand reward.

Milk Weed

Losing Control

Some live their lives from day to day
    and think they're in control.
If sickness strikes, they take a pill
    while focused on their goals.
Their ups and downs they see as thrills
    and challenges to face,
Control's maintained, or so it seems,
    'til crisis stops the pace.

Sometimes a tragic accident brings life to sudden halt.
A criminal might heartlessly destroy
    what's in life's vault.
They say they'll just start over,
    and for some this can be true;
But when their bodies fail them
    there seems far less they can do.

So much of life they take for granted is
    beyond their grip.
As passengers, they cruise but
    they're not captains of their ships.
They manage hours, days, and weeks,
    they fit their lives to plans,
But finally, they must submit
    to life's much larger plans.

Control's been lost, so they've a choice,
    they can let evil win,
But that dark choice leads just to grief
    and crying's awful din.
In such a time, the other choice is letting Jesus in.
They then find peace in trusting Him:
    Their lives complete – they win.

El Capitan in Winter

Another year

An open book begins another year,
And Christmas doesn't seem at all too near.
The football games fill ears with bursting cheers,
And quiet thoughts of Christmas
              bring some tears.

Can gifts be now so quickly lost and spent?
Can joy be quickly lost in paying rent?
Does God look down
              and know how much its meant
To me to know the joy that's heaven sent?

I wonder as I look ahead today--
To one more year of struggle day by day:
Will minds be focused just on making hay?
Or is life more than seeking higher pay?

There's hope in all of this I usually find.
There's more to life than just the daily grind.
One cannot see the future in the mind,
But play and toil release that bitter bind.

Anticipation is the fuel at hand.
We wait expectantly for luck to land
On our front doorstep just as though we planned
To make our mark on this our native land.

After the fall

After The Fall Adam blamed it on Eve —
Too many snakes in the garden said she.
After The Fall Able killed sibling Cain,
Banished to Nod, never heard from again.
After The Fall we've descended from Seth,
Living with sin from our birth to our death.

If this were all to the story my friends,
God would have wasted beginnings and ends.
After The Fall there is more to be told,
Stories that come through the ages of old,
Stories that tell of beginnings and more,
Stories that thrill us and tell what's in store.

Stories of Moses, Elijah, and Ruth
Join with the others in telling the truth,
Giving foundation for God's simple plan,
Mending the bridge from "the falling of Man."
After the Fall came a chasm so wide —
Only God's love forms the bridge to our side.

After The Fall, we were given some rules,
Binding us tight, lest we wander like fools.
Clearly, the law gave us framework for life —
Pointing towards health
               while relieving our strife.
Faith's often sterile and rigid within,
Love for God dampened by fleeing from sin.
After The Fall is a pointer to sin, but
After the fall is when winter begins.
Soon after fall, there is Christmas in store —
Bringing God's gift to our hearts and much more.
Many are looking ahead to Christ's birth —
God's antidote to The Fall for the earth.

Autumn's bright colors are prelude to Him,
Paving the way to the holidays' trims.
Meanwhile we celebrate presence and pow'r,
Noting prayers answered at just the right hour.
Life's frantic pace seems to slow for a time —
Then shopping's rushed amid music sublime.

Christ is God's antidote after The Fall —
Saving from sins all who trust Him with all.
Death's part of life, we're reminded by fall,
Colors descending from trees ever tall,
Life's sweet surrender to Him is the test,
After The Fall, Christians give Him our best!

Yosemite Valley, West Entrance

Good News

Matthew's gospel speaks with power
              born from prophets past.
Mark's more brief yet gives the reader
              images that last.
Luke wants us to see Our Lord
              through history's sheer lens,
Also speaking more to gentiles, not just Jews and men.

John, from Jesus' inner circle, sees things differently.
Talks apart from public teachings flow from memories.
John tells us of tender moments shared with just a few.
Christ emerges real and loving, intimately viewed.

Which good news we like to read
              depends upon our need.
Inspiration, facts, or change are hungers we can feed.
Jesus' teachings challenge us,
              confronts us with our sin –
Yet He can be calming, showing us the way to win.

Some may read selectively the words they want to see.
Fans instead of followers, its good they want to feel.
Then there's those who seek to be
              just like their Lord they love.
On His path, what e'er the cost,
              there's joy – and heaven above.

Tenaya Lake

Morning prayer

Now I pray me up from sleep --

My spirit flies -- get wings my feet!

It's by the grace of God above

I live out Christ's redeeming love!

Merced River

Of winter storms

The stormy winds, they blow so cold,
    our eyes can't see the sky.
We walk about with bodies numb —
    sometimes we think we'll die.
We concentrate on simple tasks, survival is our mode:
We want to do the basic things, not take on heavy loads.

We know from life's experience that storms do pass on by,
And when they've passed, we might enjoy
    a clear and cheery sky.
We seldom think of dangers past,
    our lives are filled with now.
Deliverance is just accepted,
    no "I wonder how . . . ?"

Then there's times when danger's huge
    and slaps us in the face!
We are overwhelmed with pow'r — --
    our ego's been displaced!
Stunned and humbled, weak and scared
    we lift our voice on high,
Power's holy presence brings a peace
    and then a sigh.

You and I are not alone, we look to God above.
God is watching over us so constantly with love!
In God's love we have no fear,
    for we can know God's Son;
And we can know redeeming grace —
    our stormy battles' won!

Pohono Bridge Rapids

Asking

Our asking God for what we want is
              such an easy task –
We may not get just what we want
              but always what we need.
Our prayers for things both big and small
              are easy to be asked,
Yet thanks are often not expressed –
              no sowing of faith's seed.

Some's faith is built on answers
              we soon readily can see.
Their doubts can bloom when there's delays,
              and patience often wanes.
We know that God's own timing is
              the best that there can be,
But we want swift results,
              just like avoiding life's slow lanes.

Our prayers are often puny, small,
              not worthy of God's pow'er.
We just don't ask Him God-sized prayers,
              expecting answers vast.
Not feeling worthy, we don't ask,
              and blessings are not showered,
Yet God waits for such prayers
              so He can bless us ways that last.
Sometimes our God gives dreams
              that challenge us to greater trust:
To see such dreams fulfilled
              requires those of faith to ask.
To ask God's help with hope-filled dreams
              means having faith or bust.
With God all things are possible,
              so God's up to the task.

Yosemite Falls from Glacier Point

Trust

Trust is so fragile, so easily lost –
Building needs honor and time as the cost.

Getting one's trust's an investment to make.
Breaking one's trust is a costly mistake.

Others that trust us can do so for free –
Trusting in others means trusting in me.

Trusting in God means that faith is required –
Courage is needed when life has us mired.

God is so faithful and loving and just.
God is so gracious – in God we can trust.

El Capitan on Christmas Night

Prayer

A scientific age proclaims
        the foolishness of prayer.
The media just lusts for facts
        and people's points of view.
We live our lives with stumbling steps
        and struggle, still aware
That things don't always come by chance
        or scientific cue.
So, mysticism has its place and superstition too.
And luck is less a threat than facing power
        out of sight.
So, we want power we can understand
        and keep in view.
And we want gods to be controlled
        with scientific might.
A humble person gathers scorn by those
        who relish strength.
And kneeling just is not a stance for those
        who want control.
When chaos reigns as people struggle,
        keeping fear at length,
Their comfort's sought in facts and trends
        or in opinion polls.

The ease with which a life of prayer
        is lived seems odd to some.
Unlike the lives of those who offer prayers
        when times seem right,
A life of prayer is one that lives each moment
        with the Son,
We pray and love the power found
        just walking in God's light.
There always will be some who do not
        seek the living God.
To focus on one's self is always easier for most.
To shift away from self-control,
        the concept must seem odd,
But life's a prayer for those who live
        to join the heavenly hosts,
And prayer is so much more than giving thanks
        to God above.
A prayer is even more than calling out
        in pain or fear.
Our God is waiting to forgive,
        relating just with love.
The bonding starts with prayer fulfilled,
        with God forever near.

Yosemite Falls and Historic Yosemite Chapel

Mystery, Ministry and Joy

Starting in a cabin kitchen God tugged on my sleeve.
Go, proclaim and live the gospel
            was the verse read there.
I was young in years and faith, not ready to believe.
Years would pass with other hints
            before I heard God's dare.
God did not give up on me. He even had me preach.
I was told this was my call, but I responded "no."
"Music is my call," said I. "I really want to teach."
God was patient. He was ready. I was really slow.
Wanting greater gifts to teach,
            I then went back to school.
Music history was my beat, my future seeming set.
Then came shock, life made a turn,
            and I became God's tool.
Faith became my journey,
            and my joy found in God's net.

Years have passed, and life's not been at all
            what I had planned.
God has dared, and I have lived
            as He's supplied my needs.
I've found joy in serving God,
            despite the shifting sands.
Ministry fuels hope and joy while planting Holy seeds.
Looking back, there's bonuses,
            as with God's pow'r to heal;
People taking Christ within, baptized in waters deep.
Trusting God with all of life
            does come with heaven's seal.
Joy in heaven is released when with some faith,
            we leap.

Valley View Springtime

Change

Change is what transforms our lives
        from failure to success.
Trouble comes with lack of faith
        in choices that we make.
Change feeds fear that what we've done
        will end up in a mess.
Wasting time with how we look,
        we can appear as fake.

Change that comes from growth is strong –
        begins and feeds new life.
Change that comes from endings
        brings new vision and new hope.
Confidence is born from faith
        that God will help with strife.
Certainty in God affects ability to cope.

Change is part of life and growth –
        without it we are dead.
All of this God guides with grace,
        redeems with holy love.
Change and growth in life are food
        with which our souls are fed.
Jesus shows the way of change
        that leads to God above.

Across the Meadow to the Three Brothers

Walking in faith

Walking in faith is a challenge for fools
           and the brave. There are
Those who can see beyond sight, but
           we cannot trust those who seem
Fixed on their egos and lusts. That is
           what they become — they are
Self-centered czars of their
           followers' oft' shattered dreams.

Walking in faith with Our Lord Jesus Christ
           is for those who can
Let go of pride and find peace
           in submitting their will, and who
Seek to please only the One who redeems.
           There are those who can
Do this and walk not by sight, —
           but by faith and love too.

Walk not by sight but by faith we are told.
           We can hear and see
Miles of temptation to lure us
           to logic and safety. So
Much of our life is distorted
           by short sighted values. We
Need to believe that there's
           Someone in charge here below.

Walking in faith is for those who are
           foolish enough to be
Trusting in God and in that which
           they cannot see. Then they find
That which is holy released in their humbleness,
           setting free
Power and clearing the ears
           and the eyes of the blind.

Walking in faith is the excellent choice
           for the people who
Suffer rejection and failure and loss.
           It is not for the
People who live perfect lives,
           for insensitive ones, those who
Think they're in charge. It's for those
           whom the cross has set free.

Across Curry Meadow to Half Dome

Possibilities

From flash of birth we're taught just what we can
                and cannot do.
We learn our limits and our gifts
                while gaining height and weight.
Our minds are shaped, our spirits too,
                by what we hear and view.
Our limits are not fences – rather guardrails to our fate.

The Bible says we're sinners all,
                we cannot help but sin,
But we deceive ourselves to think
                we simply can be good.
In fact, we're stained by sin,
                and deeds of goodness cannot win
Our entrance into heaven,
                but through Christ we can and would.

Our gifts and limits are not all
                that shapes our future's path.
Our God makes all things possible,
                to make amazing life,
When we surrender to His will,
                escaping from His wrath.
Our lives can soar above life's pains,
                delivered from our strife.

My friends, there are no limits
                when with God we do His will.
With trust in God, the path we trod,
                when done without a whine,
We can accomplish what we plan,
                and there's no bitter pill.
Our lives can fill with miracles
                and wondrous joy divine
.

The Grizzly Giant

Some time has passed

Some time has passed since terror changed
        our sense of who we are.
As buildings fell and lives were lost,
        the news spread fast and far.
Our anger rose as innocence was lost
        in grief and pain,
Yet courage and compassion rose
        amidst destruction's gain.

Our world is not so civilized
        that madness can't emerge.
There're always those who bear a grudge
        with anger they can't purge.
There's those who cannot bear
        to see a smile upon a face –
They're jealous of the joy of others
        in our human race.

Some time has passed since people cried
        in terror "Oh, my God!"
Some time has passed since all shed tears
        as terror touched our sod.
Some time has passed since sickness
        claimed religion as its base.
Some time has passed, we've time to ponder
        what we really face.

The enemy we face is not a nation or a creed.
We face a threat to liberty
        and freedom's precious seed.
Such seed yields hope that burns
        and fuels our vict'ry and success.
Our progress as a people rests
        on working for the best.

The enemy we face is not a people, creed or race.
We fight the crimes of infamy,
        it's justice we embrace.
There comes a time when morals count,
        when values light our trail.
Some time has passed, and with God's help
        God's justice will prevail.

Bridal Veil Fall Park

Valentine

"I love you," said he, in a tone a bit low.

"You can't really mean that — I'm one you don't know!"

"I love you," said he; I began to get mad.

"You're just like the rest, and your love is a fad!"

"I love you," said he, without hearing my sneer.

"Stop it! Don't say that! Don't write it! You hear?"

"I love you," said he, his chant missed not a note.

"Just stop it! I'll jail you! I'll hurt you, you know!"

"I love you," said he as his hands became pierced.

"It's over!" I thought, anger no longer fierce.

"I love you," said he -- echoes still seemed to ring . . .

And this just a prelude to my time to sing!

Half Dome at Sunset from Sentinel Bridge

Divine Love

Disciple Paul says love is patient
              – that is surely true.
Were God not patient, we'd no chance
              to live our lives out full.
Our verdict would be final and
              we'd have our sentence due –
But God in fact does love us,
              giving facts for us to mull.

God's love is kind, for which we're thankful,
              if we think it out.
Real love's not jealous, nor is boastful,
              and is never rude.

Love does not force itself on others,
              nor give bitter shouts.
Love finds no joy in wrongs and
              will maintain a pleasant mood.

Real love finds pleasure in the truth,
              puts up with all and all.
Through God real love will always trust,
              endure and hold out hope.
Real love flows from our living God
              says the Apostle Paul.
Like God, such love just does not end
              and fuels our lasting hope.

Lupin in the Valley in May

He walked in beauty

He walked in beauty in the days
Of healing sick and binding wounds;
And all his loving, healing ways
Were put to death and dark and gloom.
Then all the joys that loving pays
Came at the dawn — an empty tomb.

One day the more, one nail the less
Would not impair the guageless grace
Which came from God that day to bless:
For through that window we do face
Our God. So, hear our voice confess
That Jesus Christ fills us with grace.

And on that hill, and in that tomb
So still, so stark, so eloquent:
The sounds of silent victory loom
That tell of God's great power spent
Dispelling death and darkness' gloom,
That tells of life that never ends!

Trees and Moss Along the Merced River in Happy Isles

Actors

To be a Christian actor means to be a fool for God.
Successful actors don't get caught
               at filling out their roles.
Imaginary circumstances lay the stage or sod
For being truthful to the setting, momentary souls.

To be on stage is actually life we live from day to day.
Our stage may take us anywhere, on any path we trod.
Non-actors do not recognize that all of life's a play.
The key is to be faithful to ourselves and to our God.

To be a fool for Jesus' sake's a truly wondrous call.
And even without miracles our power's from above.
No matter where the script may take us,
               He won't let us fall.
We're sinners all, but when we're His,
               He saves us with His love.

Squirrel at Glacier Point

Salt

God plans for us at our beginning,

But always we spoil things by sinning.

We're always at fault,

But Christ says we're salt,

So, through Him we will always be winning.

Chipmunks at Glacier Point

Connecting spirits

Just how do people's spirits touch?
        I've wondered now and then.
One lady's letters always came expected,
        since all while
She wrote my mind was filled
        with many thoughts of her, so then
The letter came a few days later --
        opened with a smile.

So many people think that such
        connections are somehow
A psychic indication of another world of time
And space that science cannot measure
        or conjecture how.
I only know that such events
        bring warmth and joy sublime.

Just how do people's spirits touch?
        There's answers for the brave.
A leap of faith reveals
        the Holy Spirit's linking role.
We know of prayer's connective power,
        know that lives are saved
When people pray together --
        it is more than words and souls.

So, some of us of faith think
        such connections are somehow
A holy indication of a God who simply cares.
Such Holy Love connects two people,
        not revealing how
Relationships of joy are somehow built
        by those who dare.

Black Oak in Cook's Meadow

Light

We all know that evil can bite.
We can't always trust in our sight.
With darkness close in
We're tempted to sin,
But Jesus says we are the light.

Valley View Panorama

Waiting

Each one of us that walks this earth
    finds slower times we hate.
We find our lives suspended, stopped -
    directionless we wait.
At first, we rest, relieved that life
    has made some time to breathe.
Too soon we're bored, fed up, and irked --
    our anger seems to seethe.

As those of faith we turn to prayer,
    we seek some holy skill
To energize our search for goals,
    or better still, God's will.
We want to give God orders,
    but we know that doesn't work.
Our patience thins, our egos droop,
    our vision's lost in murk.

We question why, we wonder how
    our lives can stand so still.
Around us yet the world moves on,
    our wait's a bitter pill.
Somewhere amidst all this we find
    there's more than time to think.
We realize there's time to heal,
    we're nowhere near the brink.

Some waiting's ours because we're wrong
    or having gone too far.
Some waiting's ours because
    we're not prepared or up to par.
Some waiting's ours because we've lost
    our bearings and our way.
Some waiting's ours because we're holding
    circumstance at bay.

Let waiting be a chance to heal
    some friendships torn and tossed.
Let waiting be a chance to nurture
    passions almost lost.
Let waiting be a time of growth,
    to nurture faith and love.
Let waiting be a time well spent
    in seeking God above.

Watching

Each one of us that walks this earth
    finds brilliant times we love.
We see our lives so clearly strong
    and blessed by God above.
At first, we stop with awe and thanks,
    but then proceed with zest.
Inspired, there's nothing small or great
    that keeps us from our best.

At other times our way seems dark --
    we strive to keep awake.
Our zest's been tapped, our best's been tried --
    no path seems ours to take.
Our ears are pricked are eyes are focused
    out beyond our scope.
Our watching's ache's just bearable
    with faith that's fueled with hope.

Our watching's painful when we wait
    as loved ones fade and die.
Our watching's painful when the truth
    is scorned with someone's lie.
Our watching's mad when scheming foes
    don't care what conflict costs.
Our watching's sad when dreams are dashed
    or when our love's been lost.

Some watching's easy on the eyes,
    when beauty comes our way.
Some watching's fun when laughter
    fills another fertile day.
Some watching's entertainment
    as we root for favorite teams.
Some watching's preparation
    for a quest to fill our dreams.

We watch because we're human, and
    we've learned that patience pays.
It's not enough to wait and hope --
    we watch for better days.
We watch because instinctively
    we know that God's above.
We watch because our world's a gift that's
    wrapped with grace and love.

Clouds' Rest and Half Dome

GOSSIPS

Gossips are subtle, self-centered, obscene, —
Brandishing words that seem gentle and clean.
Gossips seem innocent, coating their lies, —
Hiding their hatred from friends' knowing eyes.

Gossips do not see themselves as so vile.
"Exposing" their victims is done with a smile.
Cutting off arms to remove little warts —
Seems to the gossips a comfortable sport.

Gossips tell everyone all, so they may —
Hold up their victims that others may pray.
Gossips strip clothing from victims with glee, —
Goosebumps from cold then are shown, all to see.

Gossips are fueled by the pain they employ, —
Whispering insults in lopsided joy.
Gossips carve victims with hatred outpoured, —
Building up walls
          'tween themselves and their Lord.

Tongues are a fire, says the writer of James.
Tongues can defile the whole body with flames.
Gossips build bridges of hatred to Hell, —
Walking its path but not hearing its bell.

Gossips inflict without pause for remorse, —
Trampling their victims
          while setting their course, —
Auctioning souls of their victims to sell, —
Looking toward heaven
          while stumbling toward Hell.

Gossips need Holy forgiveness from God.
Penitence — real — brings a sigh and a nod.
Logs in their own eyes, — lets pray that they see.
Then 'twill be better for you and for me!

Half Dome and Waterfalls Staircase

Hope

Living in fear we can't cope.

Living unhappy we mope.

Trusting in God

Is the path that we trod

Because hope that is seen is not hope.

Living in joy we can cope —

Faith conquers our steepest slope!

Trusting in God

Is the path that we trod,

For we're living in joy, faith and hope.

El Capitan Above the Merced River

Children of God

People seeking God the first time often are amazed.
Can it be they ask themselves that God will all forgive?
Great and lavish is God's love, His children could be dazed.
Walking in God's love, they're taught by Jesus how to live.

The Merced River at Valley View

LIVING IN THE VINE

As followers of Jesus we are
        branches of His vine.
He wants His branches to bear fruit,
        for that's the thriving life.
When we bear fruit, we're pruned to bear
        more fruit on down the line.
When we don't bear His fruit we're trimmed,
        and no one wants that strife.

We're cleaned already by His word,
        His testimony's clear.
His followers live in His vine,
        the fruit comes from His being.
We can't bear fruit without His vine,
        His love for us is dear.
We bear His fruit, His life in us,
        His love in us is seen.

When living in His vine abundant fruit
        then comes from us –
Our fruit's empowered by His life,
        we're flavored by His joy.

We can't bear fruit without Him,
        our own efforts just a fuss;
Without His joy and love within,
        our fruit's a worthless toy.

Those fans who aren't His followers,
        just don't live in His vine.
The branches of His fans just don't bear fruit
        and have no worth.
However big the fruitless branches,
        beautiful or fine.
They disappoint The Father
        and are sent back into earth.

When followers live in His vine,
        His words live in our hearts.
Our prayers can ask for anything
        reflecting His pure life.
His answers come reflecting Him,
        for we have done our part.
Our fruit is born from His true vine,
        the truly Christian life.

Stars Valley View Sky

Now

Impatiently we want things now,
        the time for waiting's never been.
It seems that everything we do
        is sensitive to timing's pen.
This pen's a cage without a door, and
        nothing's right outside its bars.
Yet from the vantage point of God there are
        no bars, there's only stars.

The now of God is never caged
        or bound by circumstance of law.
The thought of God is polished substance
        even though created raw.
The word of God is now and whole,
        created without timing's cage.
The now of God is flawless joy,
        without the need to turn a page.

Tomorrow's needs will come in time,
        and yesterdays will always press.
The needs of yesterday were either solved
        or added to our mess.

The needs of now are quicker solved
        when yesterday is in the past.
The now with which we work at last
        cannot be measured slow or fast.

Impatiently we want things now,
        not hearing "no" or even "slow."
With time there's opportunity to wait
        for now and simply grow.
When wisdom comes, the now gives way
        to slowly finding what has been.
Such wisdom finds such strength for now that
        future's joy looks back at "then."

When life on earth is done and there is simply
        no more now to face,
I think the loss of time's firm bars
        will edify God's holy grace.
When death is passed, and life's set free
        to soar through all eternity,
I think I'll see the now of God
        as love fulfilled with joyful glee.

Yosemite Falls from Cook's Meadow

THE FRIENDS OF CHRIST

Friendship is not learned in classes,
        but it must be learned.
Friends walk with you through the flames,
        e'en though they may be burned.
Friends will know you through and through
        and love you anyway.
Being friends means all of this,
        and trusting all the way.

Walking with the Lord of Life means
        walking with a friend.
Unlike us He's always faithful,
        right up through the end.

When we're at our lowest He is
        somehow always there,
Giving us what's needed,
        and supplying what is fair.

Jesus grants us freedom, we can be
        ourselves —but more.
His way is often harder,
        but rewards are great in store.
Friends with Christ give of themselves
        with efforts great and small.
Friends with Jesus find His love's
        the greatest prize of all.

Snow Flower

Fruits & Nuts

When God created all we are
        and all creation too,
Our needs were met, within our reach,
        with little work to do.
Our hungers filled with fruits and nuts,
        we had no cause to doubt
Why God had placed a limit
        on what life is all about.

Our simple lives and diet told
        of life so innocent--
We had no cares, our needs were met,
        for all was heaven sent.
Our lives were rich and full of joy --
        we lived off of the land.
But then a kind of nut entranced us
        with a fruit that's banned.

We think of fruit that comes from vines,
        from bushes, and from trees,
We think in terms of what we eat
        and not what others see.

Our fruit from us has strength to alter lives
        and change our fate.
Our fruit's our mark of excellence --
        or poison from our hate.

The fruit of God is joy and love,
        God's role for us is cast:
God's very nature's filled with hope --
        God's dreams for us are vast.
The Other's fruit is fickle,
        and its taste is often sour.
Temptation's fruit is charming,
        but it's consequences dour.

We're all just branches, you and I,
        our fruits are how we're known.
When people taste and see our fruit they know
        what seed's been sown.
We cling as branches to Our Vine --
        His being all that's true --
And when our harvest comes
        we'll still be His in heaven too.

Tenaya Valley from Glacier Point

Courage

Courage in the midst of fear is
        vital for the brave.
Lives are saved, are spent, or both
        when fear is set aside.
This one virtue can emerge when
        lives need to be saved,
Making others more important
        than our precious hide.

Other virtues, when they're tested,
        lean on courage strong.
Honesty and purity need
        courage to be held.
Diligence and kindness need some
        courage when seems "wrong."
Expressions of humility need
        courage deeply held.

Courage from just one is a majority, and more.
Brave souls win against a thousand
        cowards' and their hate.
Courage grows from repetitions
        of the past in store,
And a brave response is better earlier than late.

Courage is a virtue that is
        cherished far and wide.
Those in uniform need courage
        just to live their call.
Sometimes courage is required
        when risk is at our side.
Courage against evil fuels
        our victories great and small.

Squirrel Resting

Thoughts at Random

To wait for God is not such easy work

I keep on hoping I've not been a jerk.

There is no hope my dreams can be fulfilled

Unless the soil of miracles is tilled.

I pray each day Christ's church will be renewed.

To nurture hope is now my spirit's food.

Prayer Is Like A Spinning Wheel

Prayer is like a steering wheel – it guides the roving mind.

It cannot be just sent-up flares to God for crises' sake.

To read of saints in scriptures feels like fuel so good to find.

We move through life and care to dare when evil's on the make.

So, prayer and power grows our faith as evil's left behind.

Purity

When Jesus says the pure in heart see God,
It's character He's wanting us to grow.
Such growth makes pure
        the path we boldly trod,
While living lives amid both friends and foes.

Some see their lives as pure, without a care,
Not thinking if their stance brings others harm.
Without a humble thought they often dare
To act as though beyond God's mighty arm.

When pure in heart a Christian dares to be
A person who fulfills God's plans and more.
Without restrictions, God then sets them free
To find God's blessings and His joy in store.

Tunnel View at Sunrise

Faith and Yosemite

While driving in the valley
    when the trees are whipping by,
The foreground in a blur while cliffs
    stand sharp against the sky,
A freedom stirs inside us
    and restores our life again,
Restoring sense of balance,
    and our lives begins to mend.

Our Half Dome urges centeredness,
    we feel our God on high.
There's feelings of our groundedness
    felt from its base to sky.
Our faith within Yosemite
    is sometimes focused here,
And prayer is sometimes faith's response
    as God is felt so near.

The waterfalls that thunder loud
    can also seem serene.
Their mists so free and pools so deep
    create a peaceful scene.

A fall's intensity can stir
    excitement to our core.
There's fascination, freedom, passion,
    energy, and more.

The valley brings a sense of wonder
    not seen anywhere,
We walk, and hike, and bike, and drive –
    and sometimes stop to stare.
The eyes of faith can sense God's love
    in beauty all around.
For most it's just refreshment 'til again
    they're homeward bound.

Be thankful for a God that gives us
    eyes to see such grace.
Be thankful for the privilege of
    enjoying such a place.
As eyes of faith look up, around,
    we call upon God's name.
There's fascination in this place of change
    that seems the same.

Other books by the author available at Amazon.com:

Christian Inspiration, Study, and Poetry

Faith and Yosemite
[Christian poetry with pictures of Yosemite]

Faith Fuel
[Meditations on the Christian faith and life]

Lasting Love
[Short Biographical Sketches]

Living for Jesus
[A Gospels Study Guide for Couples and Small Groups]

Seed Thoughts for Christian Prayer and Meditation
[Workbook]

Single Sentence Sermons
[Workbook for growing faith]

Spiritually Growing Through Prayer
[How to spiritually grow by achieving a prayer-centered life.]

Walking in Faith
[Much of the same poetry as Faith and Yosemite but without pictures]

Christian Fiction

The Camera Doctors
[Two people meet on top a famous mountain, and romance ensues.]

Casting Lots
[Christian romance and adventure set in the near future]

Deliberately Growing Spiritually
[A five-year Bible reading program for spiritual transformation.]

An Extensive Life
[The life story of a man who lived more than four hundred years.]

Empty Tomb, Full Hearts
[A Selection of Testimonies Among Those Who Saw the Risen Christ]

The Gaardian Saga
[Christian science fiction fantasy with God in a major role.]

A Nation Transformed
[A future tale of God intervening in the USA with miracles.

Prayer Warriors
[Urban adventures in a near-future continuation of Casting Lots]

Soul Mates
[Romance, the same setting as Tom's Town]

This World Is Not My Home
[Two together since high school separate to find love with others.]

[Continued]

Tom's Town
[Small town life and Christian romance]

The Warrior and the Prophet
[God has surprises and blessings for newlyweds]

Yosemite Picture Books

Ever-Changing Yosemite Valley
[Yosemite Valley is a glacially carved valley. Moment by moment, scenes change.]

Portraits of El Capitan
[El Capitan rises 3000 feet above the floor of Yosemite Valley]

Portraits of Half Dome
[Half Dome marks the east end of Yosemite Valley]

A Sense of Wonder: Yosemite
[A Christian poem about Yosemite, illustrated with pictures]

Starlight Over Yosemite
[Large pictures of Yosemite taken at night]

Yosemite Textures and Shadows
[High definition photographs of Yosemite Valley, depicting all seasons, both day and night.]

www.ingramcontent.com/pod-product-compliance
Lightning Source LLC
Chambersburg PA
CBHW042032150426
43200CB00002B/26